CORAL REEFS AND THEIR ANIMALS FRIENDS

The Great Barrier Reef
is the largest coral reef
system in the world.

Coral reefs are made up of live organisms. These organisms are tiny little animals called polyps. Coral reefs are generally found in clear, tropical oceans.

The coral reef is
one of the major
marine biomes. Around
25% of the known
marine species live
in coral reefs.

Coral
reef
ecosystems help
remove and recycle
carbon dioxide. They also
protect land from harsh
weather by absorbing
the impact from
strong waves and
storms.

Corals grow in different shapes depending on their species. Coral reefs take a very long time to grow. They grow at a rate up to 2 cm per year.

Sea anemones look like flowers but are actually animals. They are related to both jellyfish and coral.

There are
more than 1,000
sea anemone species
found throughout the
ocean. Anemones tend
to stay in the same
spot until a predator
attacks them.

Clownfish are
bright orange fish
with three vertical
white stripes down their
sides. Clownfish have a
symbiotic relationship
with sea anemone.

All clownfish are
born as males.
When the female of a
group dies the largest
male will turn itself
into a female.

Sea urchins have
globe-like shape
of the body that is
covered with large
number of long spines.
Sea Urchins have over
200 species.

Sea Urchins typically range in size from 6 to 12 cm. Their spines are about 1 to 3 cm in length.

A seahorse is a
unique fish that mainly
lives in coastal areas
of oceans and seas.
There are over 50
seahorse species.

Seahorses vary
in size from 0.6 to
14 inches in length.
Seahorses are the
slowest swimmers
in the ocean.

Turtles are reptiles. They have a hard shell that protects them like a shield, this upper shell is called a carapace and the lower shell is called a plastron.

Sea turtles can be
found throughout the
world and in every
ocean except for the
Arctic Ocean.